STEM CAREERS

ECOLOGIST

by R.J. Bailey

pogo

Ideas for Parents and Teachers

Pogo Books let children practice reading informational text while introducing them to nonfiction features such as headings, labels, sidebars, maps, and diagrams, as well as a table of contents, glossary, and index.

Carefully leveled text with a strong photo match offers early fluent readers the support they need to succeed.

Before Reading

- "Walk" through the book and point out the various nonfiction features. Ask the student what purpose each feature serves.
- Look at the glossary together. Read and discuss the words.

Read the Book

- Have the child read the book independently.
- Invite him or her to list questions that arise from reading.

After Reading

- Discuss the child's questions. Talk about how he or she might find answers to those questions.
- Prompt the child to think more. Ask: Do you know anyone who works as an ecologist? What projects has he or she been involved in? Do you have any interest in this kind of work?

Pogo Books are published by Jump!
5357 Penn Avenue South
Minneapolis, MN 55419
www.jumplibrary.com

Library of Congress Cataloging-in-Publication Data

Names: Bailey, R.J., author.
Title: Ecologist / by R.J. Bailey.
Description: Minneapolis, MN: Jump!, Inc., [2019]
Series: STEM careers | Audience: Ages 7-10
Includes bibliographical references and index.
Identifiers: LCCN 2018017617 (print)
LCCN 2018017778 (ebook)
ISBN 9781641281812 (ebook)
ISBN 9781641281805 (hardcover: alk. paper)
Subjects: LCSH: Ecology–Vocational guidance–Juvenile literature. | Ecologists–Juvenile literature.
Classification: LCC QH541.14 (ebook)
LCC QH541.14 .B3425 2018 (print) | DDC 577.023–dc23
LC record available at https://lccn.loc.gov/2018017617

Editors: Jenna Trnka and Susanne Bushman
Designer: Michelle Sonnek

Photo Credits: urfin/Shutterstock, cover (beaker); givaga/Shutterstock, cover (rock), 23 (rock); xpixel/Shutterstock, cover (grass); Kletr/Shutterstock, cover (snail); leungchopan/Shutterstock, 1 (woman); Lamyai/Shutterstock, 1 (leaf); Paul Reeves Photography/Shutterstock, 1 (butterfly); Tony Stock/Shutterstock, 3 (child); Dolly/Shutterstock, 3 (drawing); Sergiy Bykhunenko/Shutterstock, 4; Oleg Senkov/Shutterstock, 5 (foreground); Pakhnyushchy/Shutterstock, 5 (background); Dave and Les Jacobs/Superstock, 6-7; jezdicek/iStock, 8t; alysta/Shutterstock, 8b; Darcy Jardine/Shutterstock, 8-9t; Kris Wiktor/Shutterstock, 8-9b; Smit/Shutterstock, 10; goodluz/Shutterstock, 11, 16-17; Francescomoufotografo/Shutterstock, 12-13; Ivan Godal/Shutterstock, 14-15; Pro3DArtt/Shutterstock, 15; Andy Dean Photography/Shutterstock, 18; Hill Street Studios/Getty, 19; Alohaflaminggo/Shutterstock, 20-21; Michiel de Wit/Shutterstock, 23 (frog); Pixel-Shot/Shutterstock, 23 (beaker).

Printed in the United States of America at Corporate Graphics in North Mankato, Minnesota.

TABLE OF CONTENTS

CHAPTER 1
Studying Ecosystems 4

CHAPTER 2
A Day in the Life 10

CHAPTER 3
Becoming an Ecologist 18

ACTIVITIES & TOOLS
Try This! 22
Glossary 23
Index 24
To Learn More 24

CHAPTER 1

STUDYING ECOSYSTEMS

Earth is made up of living and nonliving things. Plants and animals are living things. So are we!

Nonliving things include water and soil. What else? Sunlight. **Pollution**. **Chemicals**. Ecologists study how living and nonliving things interact.

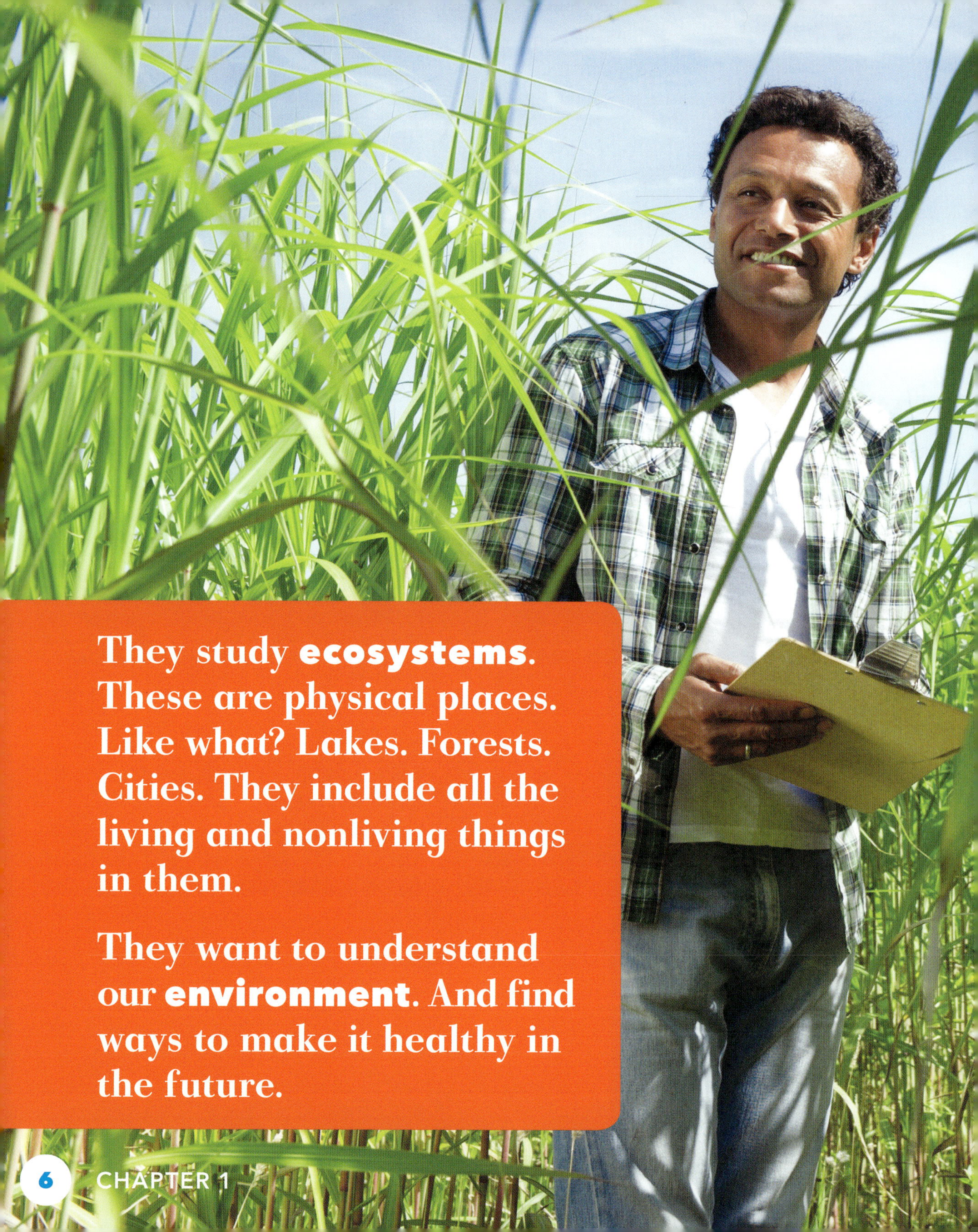

They study **ecosystems**. These are physical places. Like what? Lakes. Forests. Cities. They include all the living and nonliving things in them.

They want to understand our **environment**. And find ways to make it healthy in the future.

TAKE A LOOK!

Take a look at a lake ecosystem. All of the living and nonliving things work together. The sun is not living. But it gives **energy** to the living things. What if there was no sunlight here? How would this ecosystem change?

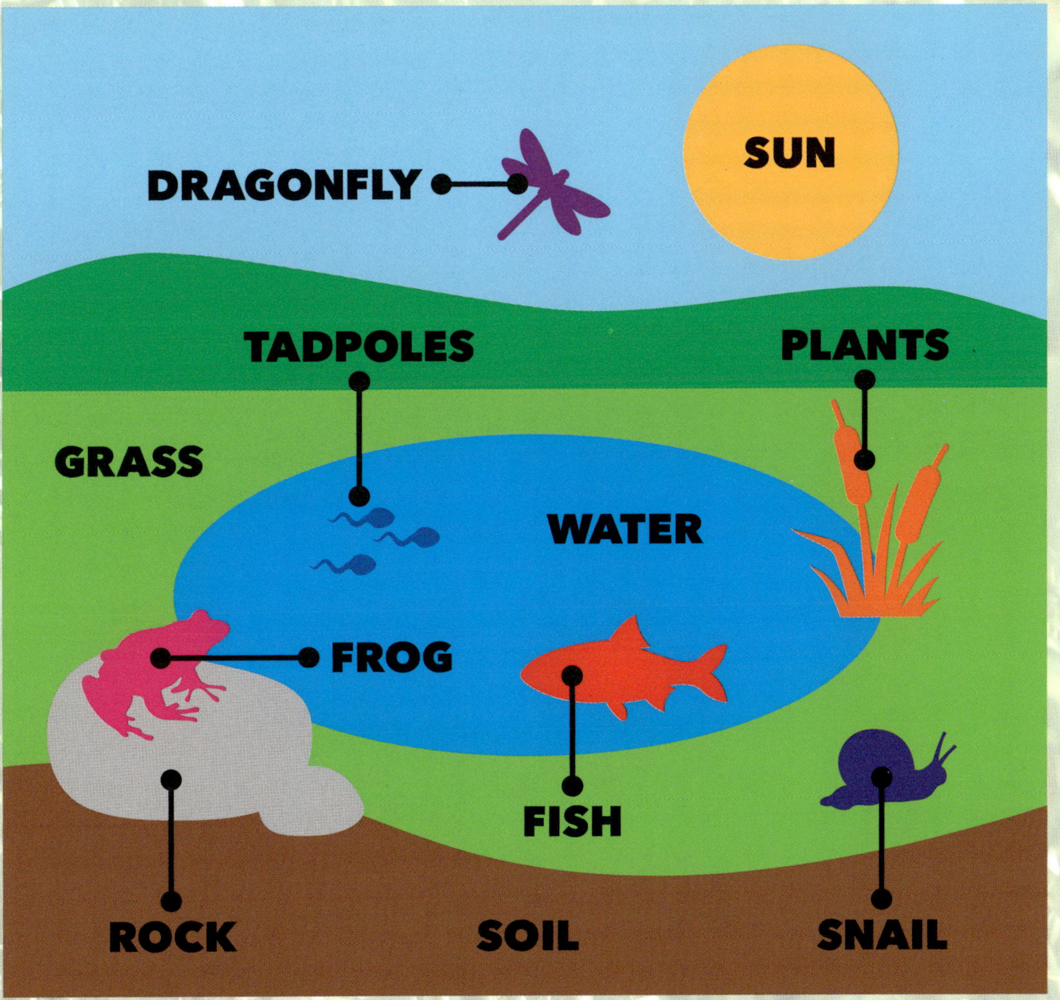

wolf

elk

trees

beaver

Ecosystems change. How? Floods can change the land. Fires can destroy it. A **species** can be wiped out.

Wolves almost disappeared from Yellowstone National Park. When? In 1995. This changed the park's ecosystem. How?

There were fewer wolves to hunt elk. The elk **population** grew too large. The elk ate too many trees. In turn, the beaver population fell. Ecologists worked with other scientists. They brought wolves to the park. The wolves hunted elk. The trees came back. The beavers did, too!

CHAPTER 2

A DAY IN THE LIFE

We use oil and coal to make energy. This causes **climate change**. Wind is a cleaner energy source. So is sunlight. But where do we put solar farms?

And wind farms? Building them can hurt wildlife. Ecologists try to find the best places.

They want to keep Earth's water, air, and soil clean. For example, chemicals can pollute lakes and rivers. They can kill fish. Ecologists work with other scientists. They test the water. They look for ways to remove bad chemicals.

DID YOU KNOW?

The water we use today has been around for a long time. How long? Millions of years! It is the same water the dinosaurs used! How is this possible? The **water cycle**.

transmitter

What tools do they need? Instruments test water and soil. Shovels help dig for soil samples. **Transmitters** track animals. Microscopes help them study tiny life forms.

DID YOU KNOW?

Ecologists help in many ways. They have found life forms that make chemicals. Other scientists can use them. For what? Treating human illnesses.

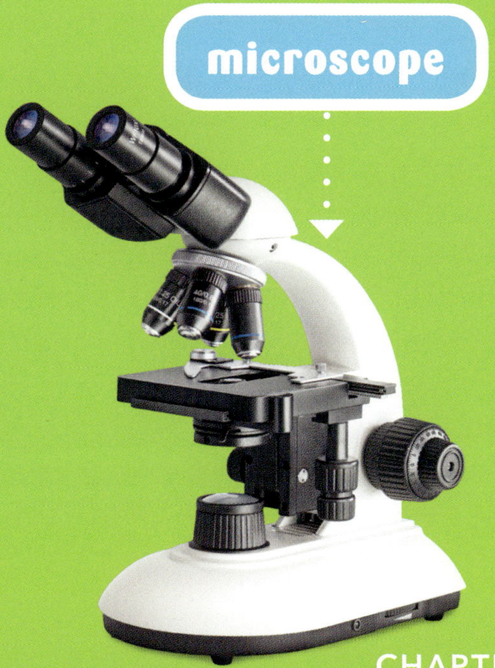

Computers help a lot, too. For what? Studying **data**. Building **computer models**. These models help **predict** how ecosystems may change over time.

CHAPTER 3

BECOMING AN ECOLOGIST

Do you want to be an ecologist? You will need computer skills. You will also need to write well. Having a curious mind will help.

Start studying **biology**. What else? **Chemistry**. And math. Plan to spend at least four years in college.

You can make a difference as an ecologist. How? You could save a species. Your findings could help improve our environment. This helps all life forms. Including us!

DID YOU KNOW?

To work as an ecologist, you need STEM skills. What does STEM stand for? Science. Technology. Engineering. Math. STEM careers are in demand. They pay well, too.

ACTIVITIES & TOOLS

TRY THIS!

A RAIN FOREST ECOSYSTEM

Water always moves. Make your own mini rain forest terrarium to understand the water cycle.

What You Need:

- large glass tank (or a 2 liter bottle cut in half)
- gravel
- charcoal
- rich potting soil or compost; enough to cover the tank floor with 1 inch of soil
- 2 or 3 tropical plants (ask your parents for help)
- spray bottle filled with water
- piece of glass that is large enough to cover the top of the tank
- clear packing tape
- notepad
- pencil

❶ **Put the gravel and charcoal in the bottom of the tank or bottle.**

❷ **Layer the potting soil or compost on top. The soil should be at least 1 inch deep.**

❸ **Dampen the soil with water.**

❹ **Plant the plants in the tank or bottle.**

❺ **Spray 10 spritzes of water into the tank or bottle.**

❻ **Place the glass over the top. You can put clear packing tape around the edges to seal it. If you are using a bottle, put the top half of the bottle on and seal your terrarium with the tape.**

❼ **Put your terrarium in a warm, sunny spot. After a few hours, record your findings. Does the glass feel warm? Where do you see water? What form is the water in? How is your terrarium like a rain forest?**

GLOSSARY

biology: The study of life and living things.

chemicals: Substances that cannot be broken down without changing into something else.

chemistry: A science that deals with the structure of substances and the changes they go through.

climate change: A change in global or regional climate patterns that are linked to the burning of fuels, such as oil, natural gas, and coal.

computer models: Representations of real-world systems or processes done on a computer to help calculate and predict.

data: Facts about something.

ecosystems: Areas that include all of the living and nonliving things within it.

energy: Usable power.

environment: The physical conditions that surround a life form.

pollution: Harmful substances that damage or contaminate the air, water, or soil.

population: The total number of something living in a certain area.

predict: To make an informed guess about future events based on observation or experience.

species: A grouping of things of the same kind and with the same name that are able to reproduce to create fertile offspring.

transmitters: Devices that send out radio signals.

water cycle: The constant movement of Earth's water.

INDEX

air 12
animals 4, 15
biology 19
chemicals 8, 12, 15
chemistry 19
climate change 10
computer models 16
data 16
Earth 4, 12
ecosystems 6, 7, 9, 16
energy 7, 10
environment 6, 21
living things 4, 5, 6, 7
microscopes 15
nonliving things 4, 5, 6, 7
plants 4
pollution 5, 12
population 9
predict 16
soil 5, 12, 15
species 9, 21
sunlight 5, 7, 10
water 5, 12, 15
water cycle 12
wildlife 11
Yellowstone National Park 9

TO LEARN MORE

Finding more information is as easy as 1, 2, 3.

1. Go to www.factsurfer.com
2. Enter "ecologist" into the search box.
3. Click the "Surf" button to see a list of websites.

FACT SURFER